OVERCOME
THE CHALLENGES OF LIFE TO LEAD TO YOUR
SUCCESS

MAME YAA

ISBN 978-1-95081-825-9 (paperback)

Copyright © 2019 by Mame Yaa

All rights reserved. No part of this publication may be reproduced, distributed, or transmitted in any form or by any means, including photocopying, recording, or other electronic or mechanical methods without the prior written permission of the publisher. For permission requests, solicit the publisher via the address below.

Rushmore Press LLC
1 888 733 9607
www.rushmorepress.com

Scripture quotations marked KJV are from the Holy Bible, King James Version (Authorized Version). First published in 1611. Quoted from the KJV Classic Reference Bible, Copyright © 1983 by Zondervan Corporation.

Scripture quotations marked NIV are taken from the Holy Bible, New International Version®. Copyright © 1973, 1978, 1984 by International Bible Society. Used by permission of Zondervan. All rights reserved. [Biblica]

Printed in the United States of America

Contents

Chapter 1: Introduction 5

Chapter 2: Challenge One
Wrong Utterances 25

Chapter 3: Challenge Two
Quarrels................................35

Chapter 4: Challenge Three
Mocking 43

Chapter 5: Challenge Four
Not Forgiving 47

Chapter 6: Challenge Five
Gossips 53

Chapter 7: Challenge Six
Fear...................................... 60

Chapter 8: Challenge Seven
           Paybacks/ Revenge............ 66

Chapter 9: 74

Chapter 10: Becoming Successful 93

Chapter 11: Moving to the Next Level.... 118

Chapter 12: Promises and
            Opportunities.................... 123

Chapter 13: Conclusion 134

INTRODUCTION

This is going to be a two book in one. First we would discuss about the challenges of life and then how that life will lead us to success in our journey of life. The purpose for this is to teach how certain challenges in our lives disturbs or stops our spiritual growth in our Christian life and when we have overcome them how mature and successful we can be.

> ➤ Without counsel plans fail, but with many advisers they succeed. Proverbs 15:22

➢ Commit your work to the LORD, and your plans will be established. Proverbs 16:3
➢ The heart of man plans his way, but the LORD establishes his steps. Proverbs 16:9

Life is like the clock or watch that ticks, it has seconds and minutes in an hour, every number in the clock strikes twice; i.e. there are AM and PM for every number. Everything we do during these times we should be careful about them. How we manage our things today may affect us some time to come or what we say today may be a trap for us tomorrow so let us be careful how we live our lives because we would account for them or face the consequences.

Being brave is not in the fight but the wisdom and understanding applied to it makes you win the fight. If you don't handle your fights and challenges well; a fight will lead to another fight and the only outcome will be chaos and confusion without a proper clear path. Otherwise Goliath would have won the fight and enslave his enemies. He had the stature and the weapons to fight and the people to back him up but David on the other hand did not have the stature and the weapons for the fight that was present and he did not have the confidence of the people yet he won because he had the right backing from the Lord and the right training to build and put his trust in him. You win the fight in yourself before you even start it otherwise you would be confused when you see your opponent and would not be able to bring out the right reaction. You acquire knowledge about the fight before you even begin. You don't just have to believe that the person who you see is the one harming you but know that there is something behind that person looking for your downfall and the only way they can get you is through this person you are vulnerable to like your wife, husband, children, friend, boss, colleagues etc. Bible said in Ephesians 6:10-18, be strong in the Lord and in the power of his might. Why? Because our struggle is not against flesh and blood- that is your brother or sister or your neighbor but the spirit that controls them is what we war against. There are so many schemes that surrounds us that are not of the Lord that war against the children of God in this life but if we do not ask for wisdom to deal with them in the Lord then we fight in vain because we would not gain the understanding to source out the cause of the problem but instead attack ourselves which results in unhappy outcomes. Our strength is not in our hands or legs or how tall or big we are but our strength is in the Lord who put the understanding and control of the problem in our minds and the power to win is in him when we put Him on, he controls the situation. The world that we are in is full of war from the fallen spirits that controls it. They direct it according to how they have planned and every plan of theirs is not one that please the Lord. Each of their scheme is against the Lord so if you are controlled by such spirits then you are not on God's side but against him. E.g. why would God tell you to smoke cigarette or drink alcohol to destroy yourself when he created you in his own image and his plan for you is to lead you to a proper end, He is not a God that set confusion. So we see that it is something that controls you to do such things that is why it becomes a sin. And God has said that we are the temple of God that his spirit dwells in so if anyone destroys the temple, He God will also destroy him. God is no respecter of persons so remember that whatever you sow that is what you will reap. To God He will give you the power to overcome but to the fallen spirits they will want to entrap you to be their slave so who would you choose to serve, God or fallen spirits. What do we struggle against then?

We struggle against things that we do not see:

- Rulers – e.g. lust, hate, sexual immorality, passions(wrong desires), idols, fame, money

Colossians 3:5 "Put to death therefore what is earthly in you: sexual immorality, impurity, passion, evil desire, and covetousness, which is idolatry."

2Timothy 2:22 "So flee youthful passions and pursue righteousness, faith, love, and peace, along with those who call on the Lord from a pure heart."

1 Thessalonians 4:3-5 "For this is the will of God, your sanctification: that you abstain from sexual immorality; that each one of you know how to control his own body in holiness and honor, not in the passion of lust like the Gentiles who do not know God."

All that is in the world—the desires of the flesh and the desires of the eyes and pride in possessions—is not from the Father but is from the world" 1John 2:16

Romans 1:28-32, And since they did not see fit to acknowledge God, God gave them up to a debased mind to do what ought not to be done. They were filled with all manner of unrighteousness, evil, covetousness, malice. They are full of envy, murder, strife, deceit, maliciousness. They are gossips, slanderers, haters of God, insolent, haughty, boastful, inventors of evil, disobedient to parents, foolish, faithless, heartless, and ruthless. Though they know God's decree that those who practice such things deserve to die, they not only do them but give approval to those who practice them

- Authorities –all authorities that is not from God in your life is from the devil so watch out.

John 10:10, The thief comes only to steal and kill and destroy. I came that they may have life and have it abundantly.

Romans 13:1, Let every person be subject to the governing authorities. For there is no authority except from God, and those that exist have been instituted by God

Matthew 28:18, And Jesus came and said to them, "All authority in heaven and on earth has been given to me

John 6:63, It is the Spirit who gives life; the flesh is no help at all. The words that I have spoken to you are spirit and life.

Revelation 12:3, And another sign appeared in heaven: behold, a great red dragon, with seven heads and ten horns, and on his heads seven diadems.

Jude 1:6, And the angels who did not stay within their own position of authority, but left their proper dwelling, he has kept in eternal chains under gloomy darkness until the judgment of the great day—

1 John 4:1, Beloved, do not believe every spirit, but test the spirits to see whether they are from God, for many false prophets have gone out into the world

Hosea 7:3, By their evil they make the king glad, and the princes by their treachery

- Powers of this world- this are the unseen powers or forces that control or influence us to do things. The tongue is one of such. There are certain forces that influence and control the mind to do something that can be good or bad. So everything we do that does not glorify God is not from God. Usually these unseen powers God's power is the best.

Colossians 1:16, For by Him all things were created, both in the heavens and on earth, visible and invisible, whether thrones or dominions or rulers or authorities--all things have been created through Him and for Him.

John 14:30, "I will not speak much more with you, for the ruler of the world is coming, and he has nothing in me;

Ephesians 2:2, In which you formerly walked according to the course of this world, according to the prince of the power of the air, of the spirit that is now working in the sons of disobedience

Daniel 10:13 "But the prince of the kingdom of Persia was withstanding me for twenty-one days; then behold, Michael, one of the chief princes, came to help me, for I had been left there with the kings of Persia.

Isaiah 24:21, So it will happen in that day, that the LORD will punish the host of heaven on high, and the kings of the earth on earth.

- Spiritual forces of evil in the heavenly realms- something that deprives you from doing what is right

James 4:7, Submit yourselves therefore to God. Resist the devil, and he will flee from you.

Ephesians 2:10, For we are his workmanship, created in Christ Jesus for good works, which God prepared beforehand, that we should walk in them

Deuteronomy 18:9-12, "When you come into the land that the LORD your God is giving you, you shall not learn to follow the abominable practices of those nations. There shall not be found among you anyone who burns his son or his daughter as an offering, anyone who practices divination or tells fortunes or interprets omens, or a sorcerer or a charmer or a medium or a necromancer or one who inquires of the dead, for whoever does these things is an abomination to the LORD. And because of these abominations the LORD your God is driving them out before you

2 Thessalonians 2:9, The coming of the lawless one is by the activity of Satan with all power and false signs and wonders

Acts 8:9-13, But there was a man named Simon, who had previously practiced magic in the city and amazed the people of Samaria, saying that he himself was somebody great. They all paid attention to him, from the least to the greatest, saying, "This man is the power of God that is called Great." And they paid attention to him because for a long time he had amazed them with his magic. But when they believed Philip as he preached good news about the kingdom of God and the name of Jesus Christ, they were baptized, both men and women. Even Simon himself believed, and after being baptized he continued with Philip. And seeing signs and great miracles performed, he was amazed

Exodus 7:10-12, So Moses and Aaron went to Pharaoh and did just as the LORD commanded. Aaron cast down his staff before Pharaoh and his servants, and it became a serpent. Then Pharaoh summoned the wise men and the sorcerers, and they, the magicians of Egypt, also did the same by their secret arts. For each man cast down his staff, and they became serpents. But Aaron's staff swallowed up their staffs

When we look deep into our lives we realize that there are things that rule over us, there are things that take control and forces us to submit whether we like it or not. There are unseen powers that control things in our world and also forces that gives us pressure to do unnecessary stuffs. But there is only one man who has authority over all and He is Jesus Christ that is why the bible says and I believe it: all powers belongs to Jesus Christ- 1Peter 5:11 so he said put on the full armor of God so that we can stand in the day of evil. Everybody have a day set aside to be tested or attacked but would we be ready when that day suddenly comes. That day can come when somebody you trusted or loved hurt you badly, or that day can come when you are attacked with sickness, divorce, marital struggles, somebody dies unexpectedly leaving you to restart your life, you run into bankruptcy suddenly, somebody cheats you etc. all these would involve somebody on that day of test, therefore how we handle these determine how prepared we are. All these happenings are spiritual not physical. Yes you see the person involved physically (actually the physical person involved is meant to bring you pain so that you would react and this would lead you to sin) but what drives the person to do these things is spiritual so if you attack the person directly you have not destroyed the source of the problem so you would have to face it again but if you attack the source and uproot it then you are free. It is like sitting in the exams class and taking a test if you don't pass you will have to retake it again till you pass and if you don't take the test you will never be moved to the next level. Whatever you do you will come to face that test again to overcome it. So when these evil days come it is expected of us to stand our grounds thus with determination:

- We should be truthful about our situation and allow the spirit of God who is truth to lead us or guide us

- We should lead a righteous life by denouncing any sin in our lives because in Isaiah 59:1-2 it says
 Surely the arm of the Lord is not too short to save, nor his ear too dull to hear. But your iniquities have separated you from your God; your sins have hidden his face from you, so that he will not hear.
- You must be able to have the peace that comes from the gospel of Jesus Christ. Everywhere you are or between you and that person (offender) learn to establish peace.
- Believe or have faith so that through the troubled times you will not give up but keep going till you reach that expected end.
- You should have confessed your sins to already be saved through our Lord

Jesus Christ so that the salvation covers you for eternal life
- Never do without the sword which is the word of God- that becomes your guide to overcome and cut through the enemy line.

Hebrews 4:12 says-

[12] For the word of God is alive and active. Sharper than any double-edged sword, it penetrates even to dividing soul and spirit, joints and marrow; it judges the thoughts and attitudes of the heart.

- Then pray in the spirit – meaning use the word of God in prayers against the forces of control because it is only the word of God that would overcome them.

Now after you have put on the whole armor- then seek for the fruit of the spirit to guide you through the journey of overcoming.

I have never said that it is easy to do these things but what is impossible with man is possible with God and with God all things are possible Luke 18: 27, Matthew 19: 26.

➢ Note that all these powers are subject to the law of God and only God can control them that is why they tremble at the mention of the name Jesus Christ because they are bounded by the laws of God.

CHALLENGE ONE
WRONG UTTERANCES

Life is like a mirror when you look at it; its blissful days are nice but when you lose it you are gone forever. Even a living dog is better than a dead lion. So let us be careful how we use it and what we do with the life we have. We can never live our life without talking or making any form of sound; usually, it is between you and somebody else. With the same good measure you want others to listen to you, you also be careful in what you say to others. Your words may be a tool to build somebody up or powerful weapon to destroy another.

Proverbs 8:8, ⁸ All the words of my mouth *are* with righteousness; nothing crooked or perverse *is* in them.

1 Samuel 1: 5-6-7, But to Hannah he gave a double portion because he loved her, and the LORD had closed her womb. ⁶ Because the LORD had closed Hannah's womb, her rival kept provoking her in order to irritate her. This went on year after year. Whenever Hannah went up to the house of the LORD, her rival provoked her till she wept and would not eat.

1 Samuel 2:3, 25, Do not keep talking so proudly or let your mouth speak such arrogance, for the Lord is a God who knows, and by him deeds are weighed.

25 If one person sins against another, God[d] may mediate for the offender; but if anyone sins against the LORD, who will intercede for them?" His sons, however, did not listen to their father's rebuke, for it was the LORD's will to put them to death

1 Samuel 3:13, 13 For I told him that I would judge his family forever because of the sin he knew about; his sons blasphemed God,[a] and he failed to restrain them

1 Samuel 10: 27, But some scoundrels said, "How can this fellow save us?" They

despised him and brought him no gifts. But Saul kept silent.

Let us watch the way we talk not let any unpleasant words come out of our mouth but only such a work as is good for improvement, teaching, learning, instruction according to the need of the moment so that it will give to those who hear. Know this that what is hidden in your heart is what come out of your mouth. All your advises are bad seeking the downfall of the other instead of seeking good for them. Be a good fountain where fresh water can always be drawn by others to drink instead of being poisonous drink where others drink and die. When before or with others you talk nice to please them but when they live you speak mean about them are you not a hypocrite.

In Matthew 12:36-37 it says

"But I tell you that every careless word that people speak, they shall give an accounting for it in the day of judgment. "For by your words you will be justified, and by your words you will be condemned."

So let us watch what we say. In Hebrews 4:12 it says:

For the word of God is living and active and sharper than any two-edged sword, and piercing as far as the division of soul and spirit, of both joints and marrow, and able to judge the thoughts and intentions of the heart.

But don't be deceived God is not mocked whatever you sow you would reap. God knows what you are already thinking before you say it so if you are mean within but smile out on your lips God knows it and would judge you. So if possible let no filthiness and silly talk or rough joking which are not fitting but let what you say rather build the other than to destroy.

- There are some their words alone when spoken will make someone want to hide because they feel worthless or even die. Words can also kill if you don't know. if you keep up with that and don't change you will be cut out by God and wisdom will be far from you.

Proverbs 3:29- Do not devise evil against your neighbor, for he trustfully dwells beside you.

Our speech should always be graceful, as though seasoned with salt, so that we would know how to respond to each person.

When we get offended it would be better to be patient about it so that we do not make the offense of the other into something else which bring trouble to our own selves. If someone offended us and we do not exercise self-control in love but try to hurt that person back through some mean words or revealing the person's secrets to hurt them and they die in the process- let me ask you – what did you gain, nothing- you may be happy for a while but you will begin to feel the guilt eat you up for the rest of your life and that person will be already gone to even make it up to you.

Proverbs 6:14- With deceit in his heart he devises evil; he continually sows discord.

If the unfortunate happens there would be hate in the heart of family members or others friends towards you and this would have led to something else. So let us learn to be patient in all things so that we would know the right resource to use to solve problems.

- Don't slander others for the offense they committed against you otherwise you will also become an offender. You the one who was offended when given the chance should teach the offender the right way to speak or how that person should have gone about the problem. But if you don't apply knowledge then you will be just like the one you accused.

- We should also watch our empty talks and boastful speeches because only God knows what would happen the next minute and tomorrow. Stop threatening people because of some background you have or some position you think you may hold; it is God who install kings and He brings them down.
- There are those who also give wrong counsels as a form of manipulating others for their gain, they have sharp tongues like swords. They aimed bitter speech as their arrow, to shoot from concealment at the blameless; suddenly they shoot at him, and do not fear. They hold fast to themselves an evil purpose; they talk of laying traps secretly; they say, "Who can see them?"'

Proverbs 25:18- Like a club or sword or sharp arrow is a man who bears false witness against his neighbor.

Know that in proverbs 13:3 it says – the one who guards his mouth preserves his life; the one who opens wide his lips comes to ruins.

CHALLENGE TWO
QUARRELS

This is acting on a disagreement or an argument between two or more people who are usually on good terms. Sometimes it involves abuse of words or in fist fights. The basis of this are anger, bitterness, envy, jealousies, rivalry, distrust etc.

These grounds for these quarrels are found in marriages, friendships, family, promotion, good backgrounds etc.

- Why do you fight and quarrel? It is because your feelings are fighting inside of you. That is why you fight.
- You want something but you cannot get it. Then you kill. You want something very much and cannot get it. So you quarrel and fight. You do not get it because you do not ask God for it.
- You ask for it, but you do not get it, because you ask in a wrong way. You want to use it for yourselves and not for others.

Don't acts on hearsays people may be jealous or envious of you or what you have and the fruitful life you may have going on. They may be looking for grounds to hurt or even destroy you so don't provide the opportunity for these. Whatever you hear from someone about you be patient about it and slow to react; it may not be true. If you are not watchful and you follow such things and act on them you may mess your good character and reputation and this will affect your friendship, marriage, happiness, clean heart, love etc. the one who wields the sword may be cut also, remember that there are those who just love to destroy things so keep watch and distance yourself if possible. If such people sin against you don't push them too far because it may turn around and harm you and you will rather end up begging for forgiveness. Learn to forgive and let it go and look for the root of the sin and uproot it. James 4:17 says if anyone, then, knows the good they ought to do and doesn't do it, it is sin for them. Also through our actions not in our speech alone can we show love therefore let us leave the judgement alone for God.

Proverbs 15:18, A hot-tempered person stirs up conflict, but the one who is patient calms a quarrel.

There may be someone who is very envious of you and want to harm you so this person may look for your weakness which may be anger or any other weakness you may have and dwell on it to get you into trouble. Your exercise of patience in Christ is what will help free yourself from this trap. When you show love through your actions you will be able to ignore such a person and look for the right channel to approach the matter and find solutions. If you rush in your anger you may act wrongly or mess up something that you will not be able to fix or may cost you something big. Always remember it is not the person but what is controlling the person towards you matters so it is that thing you have to deal with in order to help that person too. if that person chooses to let that thing control him or her and would not repent then he or she gets to be destroyed.

Proverbs 16:32, Better a patient person than a warrior, one with self-control than one who takes a city.

Ecclesiastes 7:9, Do not be quickly provoked in your spirit, for anger resides in the lap of fools.

2 Timothy 2:23-24, Don't have anything to do with foolish and stupid arguments, because you know they produce quarrels. And the Lord's servant must not be quarrelsome but must be kind to everyone, able to teach, not resentful.

Matthew 5:22, [22] But I tell you that anyone who is angry with a brother or sister will be subject to judgment. Again, anyone who says to a brother or sister, 'Raca,'[c] is answerable to the court. And anyone who says, 'You fool!' will be in danger of the fire of hell.

Proverbs 30:33, For as churning cream produces butter and as twisting the nose produces blood, so stirring up anger produces strife."

Colossians 3:7-9, ⁷ You used to walk in these ways, in the life you once lived. ⁸ But now you must also rid yourselves of all such things as these: anger, rage, malice, slander, and filthy language from your lips. ⁹ Do not lie to each other, since you have taken off your old self with its practices

Sometimes also consider your relationship with the person and ignore them, it is not everything that you have to react upon but rather be good to them so that you will benefit good things. The thing is if you are not good to such people when they are in trouble who would be there to solve or help them solve it. E.g. Your wife, child, parents, friend etc. and also when you need help critically how would they be able to come closer to give you help. They may be willing to offer the help but because of what might happen again or the thought of previous experiences might make them stop.

Note: it is not that when somebody offends you and they deserve to be punished by the laws of the land and when you are present to see it then it is wrong but it is about you that is when you are offended instead of holding it in you to the point where your own freedom is limited and you become a slave to evil thought or unhappiness then there is no sense in it but when you let it go you become free from that person and the burden involved.

CHALLENGE THREE
MOCKING

This is making fun of someone or something in a cruel way through our voice- speech, laugh, jokes, actions etc. when we mock people we make them appear stupid and take light of their seriousness.

Let us not respond to people by mocking them this may lead to harm for the both of you. For if you try to correct a mocker he would only mock more at you so ignore this person and pray for him or her they are only trying to set a trap for you. What this mocker says if you do not respond this mocker becomes the only fool available. So do not overcome evil by doing evil but overcome evil by doing what is good, for when you get angry at this person you yourself will not produce anything good to benefit from and your righteousness will not be complete. Don't continue what the fool does otherwise you will also be seen as a fool.

2 Peter 3:3, Knowing this first of all, that scoffers will come in the last days with scoffing, following their own sinful desires.

Psalm 1:1-3, Blessed is the man who walks not in the counsel of the wicked, nor stands in the way of sinners, nor sits in the seat of scoffers; but his delight is in the law of the LORD, and on his law he meditates day and night. He is like a tree planted by streams of water that yields its fruit in its season, and its leaf does not wither. In all that he does, he prospers.

Ephesians 4:29, Let no corrupting talk come out of your mouths, but only such as is good for building up, as fits the occasion, that it may give grace to those who hear.

You're a blessed person when you:

Psalm 119:1- 8-11

Blessed are those whose way is blameless, who walk in the law of the LORD!
² Blessed are those who keep his testimonies, who seek him with their whole heart,

³ who also do no wrong, but walk in his ways!

⁴ You have commanded your precepts to be kept diligently.

⁵ Oh that my ways may be steadfast in keeping your statutes!

⁶ Then I shall not be put to shame, having my eyes fixed on all your commandments.

⁷ I will praise you with an upright heart, when I learn your righteous rules.[b]

⁸ I will keep your statutes; do not utterly forsake me!

⁹ How can a young man keep his way pure? By guarding it according to your word.

¹⁰ With my whole heart I seek you; let me not wander from your commandments!

¹¹ I have stored up your word in my heart, that I might not sin against you.

CHALLENGE FOUR
NOT FORGIVING

Forgiving gives you the power to be free in your spirit and makes you stay healthy and makes you free from pain. You don't become a prisoner or be enslaved by the action that was acted against you. Forgiveness helps you to cut all the weeds around you (The weeds are the pain and negative thoughts you keep within yourself) and you begin to bear your proper fruits but if you don't forgive, whatever nourishment you receive, the weeds share them with you and so you become malnourished. Forgiveness gives you the courage to let off the past and set your mind on the future ahead.

Philippians 3:13-14, [13] Brothers, I do not consider myself yet to have taken hold of it. But one thing I do: Forgetting what is behind and straining toward what is ahead, [14] I press on toward the goal to win the prize for which God has called me heavenward in Christ Jesus.

If you don't learn to forgive others when they wrong you it will be difficult for others to forgive you when you wrong them. Somebody offended you today and you forgave know that you will also offend somebody and you will expect them to forgive you.

Remember that you the victim you are the light to shine on the offender, because everyone agrees that you did not deserved that wrong done to you, so when it is your turn to be good and instead you pay back evil for evil you will realize how the whole world would turn against you. They are trying to tell you that you don't have a right to complain when you are just the same.

Matthew 6:14-15

14 For if you forgive other people when they sin against you, your heavenly Father will also forgive you.

15 But if you do not forgive others their sins, your Father will not forgive your sins.

Colossians 3:13, **13** Bear with each other and forgive one another if any of you has a grievance against someone. Forgive as the Lord forgave you

Mark 11:25, [25] And when you stand praying, if you hold anything against anyone, forgive them, so that your Father in heaven may forgive you your sins."

Yes sometimes the offender might be doing the same thing over and over- ignore them if possible and think them as unbelievers and move on but don't forget to pray for them to change. If you begin to think negative for the person, you will not be able to forgive but instead if you feel sorry for the person who is being controlled by evil then you can forgive because you will invite God into the situation to take control. Sometimes we feel so bitter that we want to see the offender go through a certain degree of pain- but you know what when you see them in that similar pain you will feel sorry for them because you have been there before.

- Offenders, it is not good to allow yourselves to hurt others yet sometimes all you need to do is to say you are sorry and never do that again otherwise you become a slave under the act you do but you may think you are the boss yet your bad character is your boss instead.
- God is giving us a chance to exercise the mercy we received from him to others so that they can also feel his love that comes through forgiveness.
- As you are forgiving that person God reveals himself through the act by

letting your light shine before that person that your good deed will be seen and the person in turn praise God and have a repented heart.
- If don't forgive, you can't help this person or others when they are in trouble.
- You are made perfect in your weakness by God
- The offender also depends on your mercy to forgive another

CHALLENGE FIVE
GOSSIPS

Proverbs 6:16-19 says there are six things that the Lord hates but seven are an abomination to Him.

1. A Proud Look.- making a mean face or making faces at someone shows you have a bad thought about that person and you will do everything to

bring that person down when given the opportunity

Proverbs 11:12, Whoever belittles his neighbor lacks sense, but a man of understanding remains silent.

2. A Lying Tongue.- this can get someone into trouble or even kill and bring pain. Your lie can break up a home.

Proverbs 26:28, A lying tongue hates its victims, and a flattering mouth works ruin

3. Hands That Shed Innocent Blood.

4. Heart That Devises Wicked Imaginations.-watch your thoughts because God discerns into our thoughts and knows what we are planning

5. Feet That Be Swift In Running To Mischief.- don't be in a hurry to go and cause trouble God is watching you

6. A False Witness That Speak Lies.- A false witness will tell lies about other people and will also blame something they did on someone else to take the fall.

They want your spouse, your job position, your inheritance.

They'll even do it because they're jealous of your physical appearance.

Proverbs 19:5, A false witness will not go unpunished, and he who breathes out lies will not escape

Proverbs 14:5, A faithful witness does not lie, but a false witness breathes out lies

7. He That Sows Discord Among Brethren.- a person who causes two or more people to dislike or hate each other for their own gain or to get people to dislike the other

I don't know if you noticed or not but number two and number six are both liars except the liar in number six is lying as a witness to get someone else in serious trouble.

Proverbs 19:5 A false witness shall not be unpunished, and he that speak lies shall not escape.

2 Corinthians 12:20, **20** For I am afraid that when I come I may not find you as I want

you to be, and you may not find me as you want me to be. I fear that there may be discord, jealousy, fits of rage, selfish ambition, slander, gossip, arrogance and disorder.

Exodus 23:1- Do not spread false reports. Do not help a guilty person by being a malicious witness.

Leviticus 19:16- Do not go about spreading slander among your people. "'Do not do anything that endangers your neighbor's life. I am the LORD.

Proverbs 10:18- Whoever conceals hatred with lying lips and spreads slander is a fool.

Proverbs 11:13- A gossip betrays a confidence, but a trustworthy person keeps a secret.

Proverbs 16:28- A perverse person stirs up conflict, and a gossip separates close friends.

Proverbs 20:19- A gossip betrays a confidence; so avoid anyone who talks too much.

Blessed are you when people insult you, persecute you and falsely say all kinds of evil against you because of me.

Matthew 5:11

Matthew 12:36, I tell you, on the Day of Judgment people will give account for every careless word they speak

Psalm 101:5, Whoever slanders his neighbor secretly I will destroy. Whoever has a haughty look and an arrogant heart I will not endure.

Titus 3:2, To speak evil of no one, to avoid quarreling, to be gentle, and to show perfect courtesy toward all people.

Proverbs 18:8, The words of a whisperer are like delicious morsels; they go down into the inner parts of the body

CHALLENGE SIX
FEAR

Fear is an emotion which is very unpleasant; it causes pain and panic to the person it finds. Yet fear can also be good when it brings about respect towards another. Fearing something sacred gives you wisdom and understanding not to do anything that breaks the rules and the understanding of it is to know the consequences of that action. So bible said the fear of the Lord is the beginning of wisdom. It saves one from all unnecessary troubles thus it teaches us to be obedient to God's will. Fear comes when danger is sensed or when one is anxious about something. When we start suspecting ourselves unnecessarily, it poses a threat to us; we start to think the other person is out to harm us and we become too careful that in the end we in turn harm somebody else too in the process. Let us live in love work together for peace in God.

Every time we are afraid let us think of these:

Deuteronomy 31:8 "He will never leave you nor forsake you. Do not be afraid; do not be discouraged."

Romans 8:28 "And we know that in all things God works for the good of those who love him, who have been called according to his purpose."

1 John 4:18 "Perfect Love Casts Out All Fear"

Matthew 6:34- Therefore do not worry about tomorrow, for tomorrow will worry about itself. Each day has enough trouble of its own.

Psalm 23:4- Even though I walk through the darkest valley I will fear no evil, for you are with me; your rod and your staff, they comfort me.

Psalm 34:4- I sought the LORD, and he answered me; he delivered me from all my fears.

Psalm 94:19- When anxiety was great within me, your consolation brought me joy.

Psalm 56:3- "When I am afraid, I put my trust in you."

"Do not be anxious about anything, but in every situation, by prayer and petition, with thanksgiving, present your requests to God. And the peace of God, which transcends all understanding, will guard your hearts and your minds in Christ Jesus." ~ Philippians 4:6-7

"An anxious heart weighs a man down, but a kind word cheers him up."

Proverbs 12:25, Therefore do not worry about tomorrow, for tomorrow will worry about itself. Each day has enough trouble of its own." Matthew 6:34

"Do not worry about your life, what you will eat; or about your body, what you will wear. Life is more than food, and the body more than clothes. Consider the ravens: They do not sow or reap, they have no storeroom or barn; yet God feeds them. And how much more valuable you are than birds! Who of you by worrying can add a single hour to his life? Since you cannot do this very little thing, why do you worry about the rest?" Luke 12:22-26

"He who dwells in the shelter of the Most High will rest in the shadow of the Almighty. I will say of the Lord, "He is my refuge and my fortress, my God, in whom I trust."... He will cover you with his feathers, and under his wings you will find refuge; his faithfulness will be your shield and rampart. You will not fear the terror of night, nor the arrow that flies by day, nor the pestilence that stalks in the darkness, nor the plague that destroys at midday. A thousand may fall at your side, ten thousand at your right hand, but it will not come near you… For he will command his angels concerning you, to guard you in all your ways… "Because he loves me," says the Lord, "I will rescue him; I will protect him, for he acknowledges my name. He will call upon me, and I will answer him; I will be with him in trouble, I will deliver him and honor him…" from *Psalm 91:1-16*

CHAPTER 8

CHALLENGE SEVEN
PAYBACKS/ REVENGE

This is a way to get even with someone as a form of revenge. e.g. If something said something mean about you, you will want to payback by saying even meaner words about him to larger group as a form of retaliation by hurting the one who hurt you. Sometimes it is the blindness of the heart that causes the blindness of the body to lead us astray.

Know this that your revenge will only lead to more sin and un-satisfaction whiles the Lord's vengeance will lead to peace and repentance. When somebody does something to you, and you stoop to the level to do the same then there would not be any difference between the two of you. When you let go and forgive the person you block the unnecessary violence or abuse that come next but stop the sin from escalating with your calm response

1 Peter 3:9, Do not repay evil with evil or insult with insult. On the contrary, repay evil with blessing, because to this you were called so that you may inherit a blessing.

1 Thessalonians 5:15, Make sure that nobody pays back wrong for wrong, but

always strive to do what is good for each other and for everyone else.

Deuteronomy 32:35- t is mine to avenge; I will repay. In due time their foot will slip; their day of disaster is near and their doom rushes upon them."

Hebrews 10:30- For we know him who said, "It is mine to avenge; I will repay," and again, "The Lord will judge his people.

Leviticus 19:18- Do not seek revenge or bear a grudge against anyone among your people, but love your neighbor as yourself. I am the LORD

Mark 11:25- And when you stand praying, if you hold anything against anyone, forgive them, so that your Father in heaven may forgive you your sins."

Proverbs 20:22- Do not say, "I'll pay you back for this wrong!" Wait for the LORD, and he will avenge you.

Romans 13:4- For the one in authority is God's servant for your good. But if you do wrong, be afraid, for rulers do not bear the sword for no reason. They are God's servants, agents of wrath to bring punishment on the wrongdoer.

Luke 6:27-28- but to you who are listening I say: Love your enemies, do good to those who hate you, bless those who curse you, pray for those who mistreat you.

Ephesians 4:31-32- Get rid of all bitterness, rage and anger, brawling and slander, along with every form of malice. Be kind and compassionate to one another, forgiving each other, just as in Christ God forgave you.

1-peter 2:21-23- o this you were called, because Christ suffered for you, leaving you an example, that you should follow in his steps. "He committed no sin, and no deceit was found in his mouth." When they hurled their insults at him, he did not retaliate; when he suffered, he made no threats. Instead, he entrusted himself to him who judges justly.

Proverbs 25:20-22- Like one who takes away a garment on a cold day, or like vinegar poured on a wound, is one who sings songs to a heavy heart. If your enemy is hungry, give him food to eat; if he is thirsty, give him water to drink. In doing this, you will heap burning coals on his head, and the LORD will reward you.

Romans 12:17-21- o not repay anyone evil for evil. Be careful to do what is right in the eyes of everyone. If it is possible, as far as it depends on you, live at peace with everyone. Do not take revenge, my dear friends, but leave room for God's wrath, for it is written: "It is mine to avenge; I will repay," says the Lord. On the contrary: "If your enemy is hungry, feed him; if he is thirsty, give him something to drink. In doing this, you will heap burning coals on his head." Do not be overcome by evil, but overcome evil with good.

Matthew 5:40-45- And if anyone wants to sue you and take your shirt, hand over your coat as well. If anyone forces you to go one mile, go with them two miles. Give to the one who asks you, and do not turn away from the one who wants to borrow from you. "You have heard that it was said, 'Love your neighbor and hate your enemy.' But I tell you, love your enemies and pray for those who persecute you, that you may be children of your Father in heaven. He causes his sun to rise on the evil and the good, and sends rain on the righteous and the unrighteous.

You may say this is a hard thing to do but know that going through school is also hard. There are ups and downs in this journey as well. There is no school building set aside for education on life's lessons in this world so the challenges we face each day set as the class room or platform for us to pass the test. If you don't pass the test you will have to retake it again whether you like it or not and you will not see it coming mostly. There are steps to everything and if you rush on them you will fall but if you patiently take every step you will keep standing. Every time you are offended by someone, there is a power switch between you and the offender. The power of the offender now switch to the offended. Why am I saying this- there would come a time when the one who hurt you will become vulnerable to you and your time will come to pay that person back, but remember that is your test and your challenge. How you exercise this gives you either good or bad control over the situation. But if you are able to exercise good control by repaying good to the person then you have won the fight or test and you have created your reference and history in life. One that will go a long way to establish you positively in attaining a good reputation.

CHAPTER 9

This next chapter introduces us to how our success can be achieved after we overcome our challenges in life.

Proverbs 11:14- For lack of guidance a nation falls, but victory is won through many advisers.

There let us:

Trust in the LORD with all your heart, and do not lean on your own understanding. In all your ways acknowledge him, and he will make straight your paths. Proverbs 3:5–6

In our everyday life we strive hard to become successful in the things we find ourselves doing and this makes us persevere with the thoughts of attaining or reaching that goal in life and attaining it. As we wake up every single day, a goal or goals come into our minds to achieve or fulfill and by so doing we take time to work out plans and strategies to achieve them. These plans and strategies become our pathway which leads us to the success we are seeking for. (Pathway therefore means the route to; way of; access to; or way of reaching or achieving something).

There are people who become confused in life as to what their purpose here on earth is for, as well as those who look up to people to lead their lives. Remember people always make mistakes and they are not perfect, so when they make the mistakes what do we do then? That is why it is better to look up to Christ Jesus the author and finisher of our faith who can bring us to the expected end. In him there are no mistakes and he is the perfect example for our lives. Because his perfection makes us aware of where we are mistaken in our lives and then we correct them.

When King David was about to die, he gave his son Solomon the following advice: 'Do what the LORD your GOD command and follow his teachings; obey everything written in the Law of Moses. Then you will be successful, no matter what you do or where you go (1kings 2:3).

Solomon obeyed by asking God for wisdom and discernment to lead God's people, and God blessed him (1kings 3:1-14).

"My son, do not forget my teaching, but let your heart keep my commandments, for length of days and years of life and peace they will add to you. Let not steadfast love and faithfulness forsake you; bind them around your neck; write them on the tablet of your heart. So you will find favor and good success in the sight of God and man" (Proverbs 3:1-4 (ESV).

God told Joshua this: Joshua 1:7-9

"Be strong and very courageous. Be careful to obey all the law my servant Moses gave you; do not turn from it to the right or to the left, that you may be successful wherever you go. Keep this

Book of the Law always on your lips; meditate on it day and night, so that you may be careful to do everything written in it. Then you will be prosperous and successful. ⁹ Have I not commanded you? Be strong and courageous. Do not be afraid; do not be discouraged, for the LORD your God will be with you wherever you go."

Re-discovering your assignment in God in itself is success and is the first step which would catapult you to the next step.

- There are some who measure their success according to what they have, but life or success is not measured in what you have.

Proverbs 1:19- So are the ways of everyone who gains by violence; It takes away the life of its possessors.

Proverbs 16:8- Better is a little with righteousness than great income with injustice

Proverbs 21:6- The acquisition of treasures by a lying tongue is a fleeting vapor, the pursuit of death.

Then he said to them, "Watch out! Be on your guard against all kinds of greed; life does not consist in an abundance of possessions." **Luke 12:15**

To be able to be successful you must have a choice either to succeed or fail. Failure can come when you want to follow what everybody thinks is right.

I call heaven and earth to witness this day against you that I have set before your life and death, the blessings and the curses; therefore choose life, that you and your descendants may live **Deuteronomy30:19**

God wants us to be fulfilled in life by following His way ("choose life," He says in Deuteronomy 30:19). He tells us what not to eat and warns us against gluttony and overdrinking. He tells us when and where to worship and who to fellowship with. His law even covers clothing, strongly urging modesty. Its principles reach into every aspect of life.

To choose life we must judge between alternatives. Most of the judging we are permitted—indeed required—to do involve judging for ourselves which way we should go. But our area of responsibility for judging immediately narrows once we move beyond judging ourselves.

SUCCESS AS A CHOICE (SUCCEED OR FAIL)

A. Building self- esteem

Our self- esteem is the value we put on ourselves. It is the person we see when we look in the mirror. You can expect great things from people who feel good about themselves. They can push themselves and set long term goals as well as dream that everyone expects to be fulfilled. People with high self-esteem are risk takers, but more important, they are achievers.

On the other hand, people with low self-esteem are often unfocused and easily frustrated. They tend to be underachievers; they lack discipline, poor organizational skills, inability to finish things, a sense of discontent, sensitivity to criticism, envy of others.

Self-esteem comes with a catch, we must deserve it. Only when you your plan of attack, you become organized, have discipline in your life, you are prepared to win, that is when you should start to give yourself some credit.

And those whom He thus foreordained, He also called; and those whom He called, He also justified (acquitted, made righteous, putting them into right standing with Himself). And those whom He justified, He also glorified [raising them to a heavenly dignity and condition or state of being]. **Romans** 8:30

Due to this knowledge that we have in Christ Jesus, we are confident that we would make it on the success journey and that we can boost our self-esteem to make it in this life.

B. Being successful deals with your attitude, aptitude and altitude.

But the Lord said to Samuel, Look not on his appearance or at the height of his stature, for I have rejected him. For the Lord sees not as man sees; for man looks on the outward appearance, but the Lord looks on the heart. **1 Samuel** 16:7

As humans we often forget that it is God who is in control of our lives, therefore, whatever we do, we should consult him first. For He sees the intent of our hearts and he is the only one who can grant us our heart desires. Therefore we need to develop a godly attitude to approaching things, and continuously improving ourselves, as well as striving to reach higher heights.

Therefore, there is going to be an elaboration on how to build our attitude, aptitude, and altitude.

I. Attitude

The manner in which you approach any situation is crucial to the results that you ultimately achieve. If you maintain a positive attitude, you will always be able to find the upside in almost any situation. Your attitude determines your mindset; it is the foundation on which your responses sit. The attitude you choose to have will determine how effective you are.

"But my servant Caleb has a different attitude than the others have.

He has remained loyal to me, so I will bring him into the land he explored.

His descendants will possess their full share of that land."

Numbers 14:24, "If you serve Christ with this attitude, you will please God, and others will approve of you, too."

Romans 14:18, "Have this attitude in yourselves which was also in Christ Jesus, who, although He existed in the form of

God, did not regard equality with God a thing to be grasped, but emptied Himself, taking the form of a bond-servant, and being made in the likeness of men."

Philippians 2:5-7, Being loyal, and being able to please God as well as not becoming proud all deals with your heart and mind and this come about when you have a positive attitude. It is also the established way of responding to people and situations that we have learned, based on the beliefs, values and assumptions we hold. It becomes manifest through our behavior.

To maintain a positive attitude:

- Believe in choice

You must believe in your ability to choose your attitude and your responses in any given situation no matter how hard it may seem. How you respond to circumstances and the people round you is your choice. You are the master of your fate and the choices you make determine it.

- Believe in possibilities:

Make no assumptions and embraced change; this is how you believe in possibilities. When you believe in possibilities, it opens your heart and mind to new worlds; some of which you have only imagined and even the ones you have not. This mindset significantly impacts your attitude in a positive way because when you are open instead of close, your experiences are richer and you feel a whole lot better

- Believe in the future

Your attitude will be acutely affected by your hope for the future. If you have no hope, then your attitude will be one of pessimism and cynicism (distrust, doubt, scorn). If you truly have hope for the future, a better tomorrow- your attitude will reflect it and so will your choices.

The way you approach your life and outlook for the future are the fuel for a positive attitude. Without a positive attitude, it will be hard for you to imagine. A very popular misconception is that having a positive attitude is all you need to succeed while it is obvious that a positive attitude is vital to success, it cannot stand alone. If you have no clue what you what you are doing, and no plans to learn, you will achieve nothing.

You attitude is the foundation; however, your abilities determine the success in execution.

II. Aptitude

An **aptitude** is a component of a competency to do a certain kind of work at a certain level, which can also be considered "talent". Aptitudes may be physical or mental. Aptitude is not knowledge, understanding, learned or acquired abilities (skills) or attitude. The innate nature of aptitude is in contrast to achievement, which represents knowledge or ability that is gained.

Your aptitude is your inherent capacity, talent or ability to do something. Having a high aptitude for something means you are good at doing that something.

High aptitude requires:

- Keen awareness

The more aware you are the better the choices you make and the more effective you will be. It is easy to become aware of your strengths; however, becoming aware of your shortcoming is more difficult because we don't want to see ourselves in the light. It is important though to look at yourself honestly and give an accurate assessment of your abilities. The more you know what don't know, the more you will learn.

- Practices

It does truly make perfect. The more you do something the better you become at it and the more success you achieve. High aptitude comes from doing, acting on the things you learn.

- Mentorship

This goes both ways in improving aptitude. While it is vital to your personal growth and leadership that you find and follow mentors; it is equally vital that you mentor others. Although this is also a form of leading others, it can do wonders for your own personal leadership. The more you share your knowledge and experience with others, the more room you create to fill up on more knowledge and experience. One of the best ways to keep learning is to teach.

III. Altitude

Your altitude is about the heights you can grow. We all have the potential to reach tremendous heights; however, many of us wont reach half that potential. Your altitude is fueled by your attitude and aptitude. With the right mindset and consistent growth of your skill set, there are no limits to what you can achieve except the ones that we place on ourselves. Often times the biggest roadblocks we face are in our minds.

BECOMING SUCCESSFUL

Is it working hard and attaining wealth, or is it doing something good for someone else or for mankind in general? Can you be successful without being truly happy?

If success is not on your own terms, if it looks good to the world but does not feel good in your heart, it is not success at all. In the action sense is achieving something you have set out to do and it truly brings happiness and glory to God. Yet success can still be defined best on an individual basis because what one may consider successful another may consider it as a step in the right direction.

Success can be in various forms, examples are:

- It is the favorable outcome of an action
- Growing spiritually
- It is growth, development, improvement and getting better
- It is achieving what you set out to do
- Getting good grades at school
- Passing your driving test
- Getting the job you wanted
- You feel it when someone you love tells you that he or she loves you too
- It is a pleasant and powerful feeling of achievement

- Seeing your business prospering
- Promotion at work
- And many more………

God is success; therefore he has imparted success in every area of our lives: life, time, gifts, grace, promises, and opportunities.

➢ LIFE

"Love the Lord your God with all your heart and with all your soul and with all your mind and with all your strength. The second is this: 'Love your neighbor as yourself.' There is no commandment greater than these" (Mark 12:30-31).

Loving God means obeying Him and keeping His commandments (John 14:15, 23-24).

The first step in this process is accepting the free gift of eternal life offered by Jesus Christ (John 3:16). This is the beginning of true biblical success.

Once there is life there is hope, since life comes from the source who is God, we need life to attain success. So far as God is the source of our lives he gives us an inner power which serves as tools to build success. These tools are: will power, self-discipline, mind power, and power of concentration.

- Will power

This is the inner strength that prompts you to make decisions, take action, and handle goals and tasks, regardless of inner resistance, discomfort or difficulties, and this manifest as inner firmness, decisiveness, determination resolution, and persistence.

To be able to use this tool you have to submit to the Holy Spirit because he has the power to convict, admonish, teach, help in making decisions for our lives, and also sustain us through our hard times. When we give our will to God, he allows his Holy Spirit to use this tool to build our success. As it is said in proverbs 20:24: 'the lord directs our steps; so why try to understand everything along the way'?

God also admonishes us to trust in him with all our hearts and not to depend on our own understanding and also to seek his will in all that we do, and he will show us which path to take, proverbs 3:5-8.

- Self- discipline

This is the companion of will power; it endows the one possessing it with the stamina to persevere in whatever he or she does. It bestows the ability to withstand hardships and difficulties.

Self-discipline is not an easy task, no matter how faithful a Christian is. There are temptations throughout life that will constantly plague you - but if you use the Bible to help you become disciplined, these temptations won't matter as much to you. Imagine a life where you can strongly stand up to any temptation. That is completely possible through Jesus Christ. The Holy Spirit enables us to fulfill our purpose and helps us discipline our bodies through the hardships of life and through these we are able to maintain the beliefs and values in order not to sway from the truth but to use them to glorify God. Now in this self-disciplining comes the disciplining of our tongue, thoughts and hearts so that every action we take glorifies the LORD.

As the scriptures say:

And not only so, but we glory in tribulations also: knowing that tribulation works patience; **Romans 5:3**

Now no chastening for the present seems to be joyous, but grievous: nevertheless afterward it yields the peaceable fruit of righteousness to them which are exercised thereby **Hebrews 12:11**.

- Mind power

For God has not given us the spirit of fear; but of power, and of love, and of a sound mind 2Timothy 1:7

Rejoice in the Lord always; again I will say, Rejoice. Let your reasonableness be known to everyone. The Lord is at hand; do not be anxious about anything, but in everything by prayer and supplication with thanksgiving let your requests be made known to God. And the peace of God, which surpasses all understanding, will guard your hearts and your minds in Christ Jesus. Finally, brothers, whatever is true, whatever is honorable, whatever is just, whatever is pure, whatever is lovely, whatever is commendable, if there is any excellence, if there is anything worthy of praise, think about these things Philippians4:4-9

Do not be conformed to this world, but be transformed by the renewal of your mind, that by testing you may discern what is the will of God, what is good and acceptable and perfect Romans 12:2.

The mind plays an important role in achieving every kind of success and goal, minor goals or major goals. Therefore to be able to achieve these goals one must have the power to imagine in order to have the ability to form a mental image of something that is not perceived through the senses, so that one can build mental scenes, objects or events that do not exist. One cannot just get up and start creating until one has become aware of the power God has placed in him or her. But the bible said we should first of all have a renewal of mind so that we would know what the will of God is for our lives.

One may ask, what of those people who are not of God but still do great things?

Well remember it is God who gave them the power to do all those great things but at the end of the day ask yourself, do they really use it glorify God or themselves? In Genesis 15:5 remember what God told Abraham, He told Abraham to look up in the sky and count them if he can for that's how many descendants he will have. You see whenever God wants to bless us He first of all put it in our mind so that we believe and then he helps us work towards it in order for the blessings to be successful in our lives.

As human as we are, whatever we think is what we are, that is why we need God's word to fill our minds so that it rejects the negative thoughts in our minds and replace them with them positive ones and this can be done with the help of the Holy Spirit.

- Power of concentration

To be able to succeed, you need the power of concentration. It is the ability to focus the mind on one subject, object, or thought, and at the same time exclude from the mind every other unrelated thoughts, ideas, feelings, and sensations. It also means the ability to do one thing at a time, instead of jumping from one subject to another and losing attention, time and energy. Being able to concentrate the mind is crucial for success in every aspect of life, in material and financial matters, spiritual matters, and self-improvement. It helps you avoid being distracted and saves you time and energy. Concentration is needed for handling your daily affairs of life, for pursing of goals, for developing new habits and abilities, and for meditation and gaining inner peace.

➤ TIME

- Motivation

This is the driving force which helps accomplish anything; you need a driving force to accomplish your goals otherwise nothing will happen. This driving force could be your talent, idea etc. A wish is not strong enough to make you take action.

How many times have you told yourself that you are going to improve your life, but ended doing nothing?

How many times have you been dissatisfied with some aspects of your life and vowed to change them, but did not follow through with your decision?

What is holding you back, preventing you from improving your life?

It is lack of enthusiasm, motivation, desire, determination, will power and discipline. In order to get motivated to be successful, you need to know exactly what it is that you want, to possess a strong desire and to be willing to do whatever it takes to accomplish your goal.

- Affirmation

These are the positive statement that describe a desired situation and which are repeated many times, in order to impress the subconscious mind and trigger it into positive action. In order to ensure effectiveness of the affirmations, they have to be repeated with attention, conviction, interest, and desire.

Most people repeat in their minds negative words and statements concerning the situations and events in their lives, and consequently create undesirable situations. Words and statements work at both ways to build or destroy. It is the way we use them that determine whether they are going to bring good or harmful results.

But you are a chosen race, a royal priesthood, a holy nation, a people for his own possession, that you may proclaim the excellences of him who called you out of darkness into his marvelous light 1peter 2:9.

For the word of God is living and active, sharper than any two-edged sword, piercing to the division of soul and of spirit, of joints and of marrow, and discerning the thoughts and intentions of the heart Hebrews 4:12

Your word is a lamp to my feet and a light to my path Psalm 119:105.

These are all words of affirmation that one can speak into his or her life and believe that it is fulfilled. Sometimes results appear quickly, but often, more time is required. Depending on your goal, sometimes you attain immediate results, and other times it might take days, weeks, months or more. Getting results depends on several factors such as

- Time

- Focus
- Faith
- Feeling you invest in repeating your affirmations on the strength of your desire and how big or small your goal is.

Repeating positive affirmations for a few minutes, and then thinking negatively the rest of the day, neutralizes the effects of the positive words. You have to refuse to think negative thoughts, if you wish to attain positive results.

Affirmations, when repeated correctly, motivate, energize, and open your mind and eyes to opportunities that otherwise you would not have seen. It is not enough to just affirm, you also need to take action, and take advantage of opportunities that come your way.

- Positive thinking

A positive mind anticipates happiness, joy, health, and a successful result. People with positive frame of minds think about possibilities, growth, expansion and success. They expect happiness, health, love and good relationships. They think in terms of 'I can', 'I am able', and 'I will succeed'. When there are failures and obstacles they don't give up, they try again.

As the bible says, 'the joy of the Lord is my strength', therefore it is the Holy Spirit who enable us to possess this positive thinking to bring us to a success in achieving our goals.

- Achieving goals

The Lord is the author and finisher of our faith, therefore since he is going to bring us to the expected end and also since our ways are not his ways neither are our thoughts his thought, then whatever we plan to achieve, we have to submit it to God so that he gives us the ability to achieve.

Bible says, 'you can make many plans, but the lord's purpose will prevail proverbs 19:21.

Good planning and hard work lead to prosperity, but hasty shortcuts lead to poverty proverbs 21:5

It is so easy and simple to day dream and then say, 'well it is just a day dream'. It will never come true. It is so easy to give up due to lack of faith. To achieve your dreams and goals it depends on several factors

- Have a specific goal
- Be sure that you really want to achieve your goal
- Have a clear mental image of your goal
- Have a strong desire
- Disregard and reject doubts and thoughts about failure
- Show confidence and faith and perseverance until you gain success

➢ GIFTS

God has put many gifts in us such as singing, song writing, thinking clearly and logically, painting, giving, helping others no matter what the situation may be etc. We have all been given different talents, gifts, abilities. God works in different ways through each of us, and we all serve him faithfully as we use our gifts to glorify him. We should invest the gifts that God has blessed us with wisely. We should use our gifts and abilities to honor God and to bless, encourage and strengthen others **in love** (without love, all our gifts are nothing!). We should not neglect our gifts, but instead develop them, "stir them up", "fan them into flames"… so that they get even better, to the edification of the church and to the glory of God.

1 Peter 4:10-11, "Each one should use whatever gift he has received to serve others, faithfully administering God's grace in its various forms. If anyone speaks, he should do it as one speaking the very words of God. If anyone serves, he should do it with the strength God provides, so that in all things God may be praised through Jesus Christ. To him be the glory and the power for ever and ever.

Exodus 35:10, "All who are skilled among you are to come and make everything the Lord has commanded." (NIV)

Matthew 25:15a "To one he gave five talents, to another two, to another one, to each according to his ability. Then he went away." (ESV)

But it's obvious by now, isn't it, that Christ's church is a complete Body and not a gigantic, dimensional Part? It's not all Apostles, not all Prophets, not all Miracle Workers, not all Healers, not all Prayer in Tongues, not all Interpreter of Tongues. And yet some of people keep competing for so-called "important" parts.

➢ GRACE

You cannot do anything without God's grace. If grace is not part of our lives we are nothing.

We have the "goodwill" of God working through His children under this meaning. It is His favor toward us, leading us by His providence, toward those things that are best for us. Paul uses this aspect of Grace when he wrote: "But by the grace of God I am what I am: and his grace which was bestowed upon me was not in vain; but I labored more abundantly than they all: yet not I, but the grace of God which was with me." (1 Cor. 15:10).

Paul points out that we must accept this grace. We must use what God has given to us, so that God might receive the glory. Each of us are beneficiaries of this Grace. Our spiritual growth is dependent upon how we use the goodness and favor of God in our lives. How great it would be to say as Paul, that what God has done for us is "not in vain."

Grace can be likened to a time period. Grace is a time period when God gives to humanity His full mercy and favor. This time period is given so that we might be redeemed from our debt of sin. Our debt is due, yet God extends the payment period to allow us to obtain redemption. We see this principle used in modern banking. Our loan is a debt that is due every month. The day arrives, and we do not have the means to pay off that debt. The bank extends to us a short period of time in which we can redeem our debt without suffering any consequences. If we do not redeem that debt within this "grace period," then we shall suffer the consequences.

God has granted to each of us time, time in which we can redeem ourselves from our debt of sin. God has given His Son as the means by which we might redeem ourselves (John 3:16). Two circumstances will govern our own period of Grace. The first circumstance is our lifetime. We do not know how long we shall live. God gives to all men opportunities to know His will, and to obey the gospel. If we do not redeem ourselves within our lifetime, by taking advantage of God's grace, then we shall suffer the consequences - eternal life in hell.

MOVING TO THE NEXT LEVEL

To be able to move to the next level there must be a desire, intent, and a follow through to reach the level you want.

To desire to move to the next level:

You must understand your true desires in order to reach high altitudes. The more you understand what it is you truly seek, the better your choices will be, bringing you closer to your goals. With a crystallized goal in mind, your choices and actions will reflect that intensity.

Trust in the LORD and do good; dwell in the land and cultivate faithfulness. Delight yourself in the LORD; And He will give you the desires of your heart. Commit your way to the LORD,

Trust also in Him, and He will do it. Psalm 37:3-5

If we take a whole-hearted satisfaction in Jesus, he will mold and shape our hearts so that we have proper desires. In doing so, as we commit our path to He will be faithful to establish our ways before Him. We also have to trust in the lord and create a faithful habit, more over we also have to be happy in him and then in everything we do, we have to commit our ways to him so that he can direct our paths and then by so doing, he will open our eyes to see what we truly desire to achieve them.

Having intent:

Knowing what your intent is, is like an arrow heading for the bull's eye. Its purpose is clear. Desire precedes intent and intent precedes follow through. Again, it is important to truly understand exactly what your intentions are; this is your guiding light for the choices you make. You decide what to do and say based on your true intent.

If our thoughts and attitudes reflect the joy of Christ, and our outlook and personality are positive, we can work healing in many lives (<u>you are what you think</u>).

"For as he thinks in his heart, so is he." – Proverbs 23:7

If we fill our minds with ungodly words, music, images, movies, etc., then our lives will gravitate to that which is ungodly. Or in other words: "garbage in, garbage out". Alternatively, if we fill our minds with upright thoughts, good things, and the Word of God, our lives will levitate to a higher level of being. The point is that *our minds are always thinking*, and those things which we dwell on will shape our thoughts, our actions and every aspect of our lives.

Follow through:

Without action, nothing gets done. This is why it is important to follow through your plans. Personal leader ship requires that you follow through on your intent in order to achieve your goal. When your desire and intent are clear, it will help you to avoid the pitfalls of the debilitating (draining, unbearable) disease of procrastination.

CHAPTER 12

PROMISES AND OPPORTUNITIES

Delight thyself also in the LORD: and he shall give thee the desires of thy heart." "But my God shall supply all your need according to his riches in glory by Christ Jesus." (Psalm 37:4 and Philippians 4:19)

Who could ask for more assurance than these statements from God's Word itself regarding His fulfillment of our needs and desires? These two verses are both definitive statements that leave us with no doubt that we can trust God completely with all that we long for or feel in need of in our lives. Why then do we so often feel as though God has somehow backed down on His Word or overlooked us with His blessings? Much of our emotional pain concerning our singleness is a result of believing that God has withheld the fulfillment of his promises to us. There are many things we think we absolutely need. But a true need in God's eyes is anything essential for fulfilling His purposes for us and for making us whole people (spiritually healthy). A need is a true deficiency, lack or shortage of something essential in our lives.

A desire, on the other hand, is not something that is essential, but something which is enjoyable in the process of fulfilling God's purposes. It is a hankering, longing, pining or yearning for something that we would like to have to enrich our lives here on earth.

In addition to meeting our needs, God also delights in giving us our desires. But He will always give them within the parameters of what we need: if He sees that we need the freedom of singleness to fulfill His purposes, He will not fulfill our desire for sexual intimacy with another person. If He sees we need the partnership of marriage to fulfill His purposes, He will not fulfill our desire to be free of the responsibility of taking care of our family. If He sees we need the character building of suffering in our lives, He will not immediately fulfill our desire to be relieved of the pain of loss or of heartache or of physical ailment.

But I rejoiced in the Lord greatly, that now at the last your care of me hath flourished again; wherein ye were also careful, but ye lacked opportunity. Not that I speak in respect of want: for I have learned, in whatsoever state I am, therewith to be content. I know both how to be abased, and I know how to abound: everywhere and in all things I am instructed both to be full and to be hungry, both to abound and to suffer need [physical and psychological]. I can do all things through Christ which strengthened me....But my God shall supply all your need according to his riches in glory by Christ Jesus. Now unto God and our Father be glory for ever and ever. Amen. (Philippians 4:10-20)

Revelation 3:8: "I know your works. See, I have set before you an open door, and no one can shut it; for you have a little strength, have kept my word, and have not denied my name."

God opens doors in our lives for various reasons. There can be doors of opportunities and doors that lead us from one season to another. If we are obedient and allow the Holy Spirit to guide us, we begin to develop clarity to find these open doors and the courage to explore within.

The Apostle Paul spoke of open doors in the following passages …

2 Corinthians 2:12: "Furthermore, when I came to Troas to preach Christ's gospel, and a door was opened to me by the Lord."

Colossians 4:2: "Continue earnestly in prayer, being vigilant in it with thanksgiving; meanwhile praying also for us, that God would open to us a door for the word, to speak the mystery of Christ."

The doors that God opens in our lives lead to new beginnings, new blessings and new opportunities to be effective witnesses for the Lord. Jesus Christ, who awaits us at the front door of God's Salvation, is the Gate through which we walk and find life. Just as there is only one door to our heart, there is only one door to the heart of God. Let us walk without fear through God's open doors, knowing that His protection, His provision, His peace and His power will forever reside within us.

Genesis 2:15-17: The LORD God took the man and put him in the Garden of Eden to work it and take care of it. And the

LORD God commanded the man, "You are free to eat from any tree in the garden; but you must not eat from the tree of the knowledge of good and evil, for when you eat from it you will certainly die."

In the Genesis 2 creation story, the human has work and responsibility from the very beginning

God places the man in the garden "to till it and to keep it." From the beginning, humans are made for a regular rhythm of doing work that has meaning and purpose for the good of creation along with regular periods of Sabbath rest and enjoyment (Genesis 2:2-3). While there is great freedom for the human ("you may freely eat from any tree"), the garden also contains one boundary that restricts the human. God decrees the first biblical law (eating fruit from the tree of the knowledge of good and evil [or bad/pain) and the consequence of breaking the law (immediate and certain death "in the day... you shall die [the Hebrew is emphatic--you shall surely die!]" (Genesis 2:17).

The Lord God took the man. - The same omnipotent hand that made him still held him. "And put him into the garden." The original word is "caused him to rest," or dwell in the garden as an abode of peace and recreation. "To dress it and to keep it." The plants of nature, left to their own course, may degenerate and become wild through the poverty of the soil on which they alight, or the gradual exhaustion of a once rich soil. The hand of rational man, therefore, has its appropriate sphere in preparing and enriching the soil, and in distributing the seeds and training the shoots in the way most favorable for the full development of the plant, and especially of its seed or fruits. This "dressing" was needed even in the garden. The "keeping" of it may refer to the guarding of it by enclosure from the depredations of the cattle, the wild beasts, or even the smaller animals. It includes also the faithful preservation of it as a trust committed to man by his bounteous Maker. There was now a man to till the soil. The second need of the world of plants was now supplied. Gardening was the first occupation of primeval man.

In all this, God showed his love by giving us three things to guide us through our activities in life. They are:

- Independent will
- Guiding conscience
- Freedom of choice

a. Independent will

Independent will is the ability to keep the promises we make to ourselves and others. It is the ability to make decisions and choices and to act in accordance with those choices and decisions. The extent to which our independent will is developed is tested in our day-to-day lives in the form of personal integrity. It is integral part of how much value is placed on oneself. Real discipline should come from within based on your own core values and also from where they are derived.

b. Guiding Conscience

What is conscience?

Conscience is that part of the human spirit that acts as our moral guide leading us to the right actions as well as showing us when we have done something wrong. It is also an aptitude, faculty intuition or judgment of the intellect that distinguishes right from wrong. It is the voice of a person's spirit which God gave to us and thus makes us united with God.

c. Freedom of choice

CONCLUSION

God has invested so much in us that he wants and expects us to be successful in all that we do. He has invested in us life, time, gifts, grace, promises, and opportunities. More so He has given us grace in him and with the help of the Holy Spirit everything we do brings glory to his name.

In growing to become successful, God wants us to grow spiritually and be happy.

Because when we are happy in him, minor unpleasant events usually do not disturb us. When are unhappy, we feel as if everything is against us. Happiness is feeling of inner peace and satisfaction. It is usually experienced when there are no worries, fears or obsessing thoughts, and this usually happens when we do something we love to do or when we get, win, gain or achieve something that we value.

Growing spiritually brings about some benefits:

- We develop detachment, which leads to inner peace
- We learn not to let outside circumstance affect our moods and states of mind
- We become more patient and tolerant

- We learn to rise above frustration, disappointment and negative feelings
- Inner power and strength increase
- Increase feeling of happiness
- Our intuition get sharper
- We become better citizens of the world
- Our understanding of our inner essence, what we are, and why we are here grows.

Hebrews 13:20-21, [20] Now may the God of peace, who through the blood of the eternal covenant brought back from the dead our Lord Jesus, that great Shepherd of the sheep,[21] equip you with everything good for doing his will, and may he work in us what is pleasing to him, through Jesus Christ, to whom be glory for ever and ever. Amen.

www.ingramcontent.com/pod-product-compliance
Lightning Source LLC
Chambersburg PA
CBHW030118100526
44591CB00009B/447